fehler abc

English – German

von Horst Zindler
und William Barry

Zweite, durchgesehene Auflage

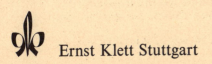

Ernst Klett Stuttgart

Contents

2. Auflage   2   56   55   54   53 | 1984   83   82   81

Die vorliegende 2. Auflage ist gegenüber der ersten Auflage stark korrigiert worden. Sie ist neben der 1. Auflage nicht verwendbar.

Alle Drucke der 2. Auflage können im Unterricht nebeneinander benutzt werden. Die letzte Zahl bezeichnet das Jahr dieses Druckes.

Druck: Wilhelm Röck, Weinsberg. Printed in Germany.
ISBN 3-12-551100-3

About this book

You have probably noticed that there are some mistakes you make time and time again in German; you find some words difficult to remember, and when you have learned them you don't know when to use them. They are as difficult to get rid of as chewing-gum from your coat. The reason: you have not been given a short, concise explanation nor the chance to practise.

This little book is intended to help you solve these difficulties.

How do you set about it?

Try doing the test on page 4, and then check your answer with the solutions given on page 82. If you make less than 15 mistakes you can consider it a good result. If you have more than 30 mistakes you have got a good deal of practice ahead of you.

Work through the individual entries either in alphabetical order or, if you wish, concentrate first on your mistakes. Translate the sentences on the left of the page into German, and compare your translation with the version on the right by placing the red transparent film, which you will find at the back of the book, over the page. Note that where the "Sie"-form for "you" is used in the German translation, the "du"-form can also be used, and vice-versa.

After doing the exercises once, or preferably several times, try doing the test again. Keep at it until you don't make any more mistakes.

We are sure that you will learn a lot by working your way through this book, and that afterwards you will be able to forget about a large number of the difficulties you are having with German at the moment.

Test-sentences

The solutions are given on p. 82.

1. Er . . . ihn um Hilfe. (asked)
2. Alte Menschen . . . selten ihre Meinung. (change)
3. Bob fährt morgen . . . die Schweiz. (to)
4. Das Leben dort ist . . . als hier. (different)
5. Die . . . der Studenten steigt. (number)
6. Sie kommen heute abend . . . . (here)
7. Das Haus . . . meinem Großvater. (belongs to)
8. . . . wir uns verabschiedet hatten, gingen wir. (after)
9. Wir trafen uns am . . . zum Kino. (entrance)
10. Weiß jemand, . . . er kommt? (if)
11. Sie können sich nicht . . . , was er gemacht hat. (imagine)
12. Ich habe . . . mit ihm telefoniert. (just)
13. . . . Sie ihn? (know)
14. Anne ist . . . sechzehn. (only)
15. Susan ist mit Fred . . . . (married)
16. Wir . . . in der Feldstraße. (live)
17. Wir . . . jeden Sonntag. (meet)
18. Wird es lange . . . ? (take)
19. Was hat Ihnen der Arzt . . . ? (prescribed)
20. . . . Sie die Flaschen bitte auf den Tisch! (put)
21. Ist noch etwas . . . im Koffer? (room)
22. Die alte Dame . . . drei Zimmer an Studenten. (rents)
23. Das . . . Sie . . . sagen! (must not)
24. Alle . . . , ihm zu helfen. (tried)
25. Wir haben im letzten Jahr viel Geld . . . . (saved)
26. Meine Uhr ist . . . . (stopped)
27. Wann hat er das Haus . . . ? (left)
28. Ich muß es noch . . . dem Frühstück tun. (before)
29. Wissen Sie, . . . er kommt? (when)
30. Ich muß . . . das Problem . . . . (think about)
31. . . . Sie mich bitte erst um 10 Uhr. (wake up)
32. Ich möchte . . . Zucker. (some)
33. Niemand weiß, . . . sie fahren wollen. (where)

4

34. Wie wollt ihr euer Kind . . . ? (call)
35. . . . Sie bitte diesen Brief zur Post. (take)
36. Im Sommer ist es schon um 5 Uhr
    morgens . . . . (light)
37. Wie . . . diese Maschine? (works)
38. . . . nur ein paar Leute im Kino. (there were)
39. Diese Flüssigkeit ist sehr gefährlich.
    Seien Sie . . . damit! (careful)
40. . . . Sie sich bitte um die Gäste. (attend)
41. An der Unfallstelle . . . viele Menschen. (gathered)
42. Ich kann es Ihnen . . . nicht geben. (I'm afraid)
43. Sagen Sie es bitte . . . . (again)
44. Er hat es niemandem gesagt . . . mir. (but)
45. Die Firma wurde . . . meinem Vater (by)
    gegründet.
46. Was . . . das? (mean)
47. Mein . . . war schon besetzt. (seat)
48. Ich . . . , was Sie meinen. (see)
49. Er sagte . . . . (so)
50. Stellen Sie das Glas bitte nicht . . . . (there)

List of English Headwords

with page number

1. to admit

zugeben — to acknowledge or confess
zulassen — to allow to enter, to let in

You must admit that he's
not quite as stupid as he
looks.

Children under twelve are
not admitted.

He admitted his error.

We only admit club-
members to our meetings.

2. to be afraid

Angst haben (vor) — to be afraid (of)
Ich fürchte, . . . — I'm afraid (in anticipation of s.th.
                        unpleasant)
leider — I'm afraid; unfortunately

Don't be afraid!

I'm afraid you'll get into
trouble.

I'm afraid we'll be late.

Thomas is afraid of dogs.

I'm afraid I don't know.

I'm afraid he'll have
to do it again.

I'm afraid I can't
help you.

3. after

nach + noun — (temporal preposition)
nachdem + verb — (temporal conjunction)
danach, hinterher, nachher — after that, afterwards

After he had eaten something he ordered a cup of tea.

What are we going to do after that?

After supper they went to the cinema.

After he had paid the bill, he left the restaurant.

He couldn't work after the accident.

First she went shopping, and after that she visited her boyfriend.

Note:

In colloquial speech *hinter . . . her* means "in pursuit of s.o. or s.th".

I've heard that the police are after him.

4. again

wieder — back in the original condition, position etc
noch einmal — once more

Please do it again!

After ten minutes rest
she felt better again.

I'm not going to say it
again.

It's nice to be home again.

Note:

never again — *nie wieder*

I promise I'll never do it
again.

5. another

noch ein(-e) — one more, an additional (one)
ein anderer(-es), eine andere — a different (one)

Another beer, please!

Another waiter served
the food.

Would you like another
orange?

Could you give me another
screwdriver? This one is
too small.

Note:

another one

noch einer, noch eins, noch eine — an additional one
ein anderer(-es), eine andere — a different one

That ice-cream was good;
I want another one.

This knife is dirty. Bring
me another one, please.

6. to be anxious

besorgt sein (um) — to be worried (about)
unbedingt wollen — to want very much

He was anxious to speak
to the manager.

Mrs Turner was very
anxious about her sick
daughter.

She was anxious to be
there on time.

Whenever Peter stayed out
late, his parents were
very anxious.

7. to appear

scheinen — to seem
erscheinen — to come into sight

He doesn't appear to have
any time for his family.

We were both glad when
the bus finally appeared.

He doesn't appear to
recognize me.

You appear to find German
difficult.

Suddenly a dark figure
appeared at the window.

8. to arrange

ordnen — to put in order
vereinbaren — to make arrangements; to come to an
agreement

Barbara arranged
the flowers in the vase.

They arranged
a meeting-place.

The books were arranged
alphabetically.

We forgot
to arrange a time.

Note:

to arrange to meet s.o. — *sich mit jdm verabreden*

He arranged to meet her
at 8 o'clock.

12

9. as

als { in the function of
     when, while
wie — (introducing non-defining relative clause)
weil, da — because

As Mayor he felt respon-
sible for it.

I went home at once, as
it was rather late.

As everybody knows, time
solves all problems.

As a young girl she was
very pretty.

Berlin was exactly as
I remembered it.

The telephone rang as I
was about to have lunch.

We all went to bed early,
as we had a hard day
ahead of us.

I saw her as she came out
of the house.

Note:

as . . . as — *so . . . wie*
not so/as . . . as — *nicht so . . . wie*

He isn't as healthy as
he was.

She is as pretty as
her mother.

13

10. to ask

bitten um + noun — to ask for s.th.
bitten + *zu* + inf — to ask (s.o.) to (do s.th.)
einladen (zu) — to ask to come, to invite
fragen nach { to ask about, to inquire about
to ask (e.g. the time, the way)

He asked him for a light.

He asked his friends to supper.

The student asked about the books he needed.

The tourist asked the policeman to help him.

The little boy asked me the time.

He asked his friend to lend him £40.

11. to attend

zuhören + dat — to attend to what s.o. says, to listen carefully
sich kümmern um — to give attention to
teilnehmen an + dat — to be present, to take part

He wasn't attending to what the guide said.

Fifteen students attended the course last term.

Who is attending to our luggage?

He couldn't attend the last meeting.

Please attend to your work!

You're not attending!

Note:

Are you being attended to? — *Werden Sie bedient?*

12. to avoid

meiden — to avoid coming into contact with a person or thing
vermeiden — not to let something happen

They naturally wanted to avoid a scandal.

I have a feeling she's avoiding me.

The doctor advised him to avoid alcohol.

The star wanted to avoid being seen.

It's better to avoid the motorway on Sundays.

13. before

vor + noun — (temporal preposition)
bevor + verb — (temporal conjunction)
vorher — before that, previously
schon einmal — (once) before, already

Have you done that
before?

Before I came to Germany,
I couldn't speak
a word of German.

He's in Austria now.
Before, he was in Spain.

Do you want to hear the
news before supper?

He always goes for a walk
before he goes to bed.

Have you read
that book before?

I can't do anything
before breakfast.

I would have told him
before.

14. to belong to

gehören + dat — to be the property of
gehören zu + dat — to go with, to be part of, to be a
member of

The car belongs
to my father.

This key belongs
to the cupboard.

Does this wallet
belong to you?

He belongs to our
yacht-club.

Note:

The flowers belong in the living-room. — Die Blumen
gehören ins Wohnzimmer.

15. bright

hell — bright (of light)
hell (colloquial) — intelligent
leuchtend — bright (of colours, eyes)

She always wears bright
colours.

This lamp is too bright
for me.

His nose was bright red.

He's a bright fellow.

16. busy

beschäftigt — having a lot to do (refers to persons)
lebhaft — full of people, life, movement, traffic
(refers to places and situations)

Politicians are always
very busy.

We live in a very
busy street.

He's very busy again
today.

The accident occurred
at a busy junction.

Note:

lebhaft (refering to people) — lively

Teachers like
lively children.

17. but

aber — (conjunction)
sondern — (conjunction; introduces a positive statement
contradicting a preceding negative one)
außer — except (preposition)

I don't trust anyone
but you.

It was very late but he
didn't want to get up.

It wasn't in 1956 but in
1957 that Peter and Mary
got married.

He spoke very softly but everybody understood him.

Everyone but me was invited.

There's nothing to eat but cheese.

Note:

nicht nur . . . sondern auch — not only . . . (but) . . . also

That isn't only difficult, it's also dangerous.

18. by

an — near, by the side of
bis (spätestens) — not later than
von (with passive) — (done) by s.o. or s.th.

My grandmother lives by the sea.

This tree was planted by my grandfather.

We must be home by 8 o'clock.

America was discovered by Columbus.

They met by the church.

Can you give me the book back by Friday?

Note:

by car, train, plane etc — *mit* dem Auto, Zug, Flugzeug etc
to learn by heart — *auswendig* lernen

19. to call

heißen — to be called, to have the name . . .
nennen — to give a name to
rufen — to shout, to address s.o.
anrufen — to call (up), to phone

She asked me to call her during the afternoon.

They called their youngest son Benjamin.

Mark called her name, but she didn't answer.

What's Venice called in Italian?

My mother called me back.

You call that art!?

The driver is badly hurt. We must call a doctor immediately.

The Queen's residence in London is called "Buckingham Palace".

Note:

besuchen — to call on, to visit
abholen — to call for

Can you call for me at 7 o'clock?

He said I could call on him any time.

Yesterday evening an old
friend called on me.

Elizabeth calls for me
on the way to work
every morning.

20. careful(ly)

vorsichtig — cautious(ly)
  (in order to avoid unpleasant consequences)
sorgfältig — painstaking(ly)
  (in order to achieve the best possible results)

Be careful; don't
burn yourself!

The police carefully
removed the bomb.

The plan has to be
carefully worked out.

Eggs have to be packed
and transported carefully.

He's known for his
careful work.

21. to change

1. Something is exchanged for something else.

sich umziehen — to change (one's) clothes
umsteigen — to change from one vehicle to another
wechseln — to exchange one for another (e.g. money, job, subject)

This pullover is too warm, I must change.

Can you change ten marks for me?

I must change before we go out.

You must change at Hanover.

He has never changed his job.

We had to change from the bus to the train.

2. Something/someone changes or is changed.

(sich) ändern — to alter, to become or to make different (e.g. decision, direction, opinion)
(sich) verwandeln — to transform completely

He's constantly changing his plans.

The frog changed into a prince.

You can't change water into wine.

When he heard that he changed his opinion.

22. to complain

klagen
meckern (colloquial) } to express dissatisfaction
sich beschweren — to make a complaint

Everybody is complaining about the weather.

The customer complained to the manager about the bad service.

There are always people who complain.

The old lady complained to the neighbours about the noise.

23. to cry

schreien — to cry out
weinen — to weep

Helga is terribly depressed. She cries all day long.

Don't cry, it'll be all right.

Sometimes you don't know why a baby is crying.

He cried, "Help!" But nobody heard him.

24. to decide

sich entschließen — to decide for or against a given possibility
(sich) entscheiden — to decide on one of two or more
possibilities

I've decided to buy a car.

My wife will decide
what kind.

He has decided to
emigrate.

He hasn't yet decided
on a country.

We have decided to go
on holiday.

We haven't yet decided
where.

Note:

Er *ist entschlossen,* es zu tun. — He is determined to do it.

Kurz entschlossen fuhr er ab. — He left on the spur of the
moment.

25. to deny

verweigern — to refuse to give/grant
leugnen — to dispute/contest a statement or accusation

The accused denies
knowing anything about
the bank robbery.

They deny their children
nothing.

He wanted to go to Russia,
but he was denied a visa.

You can't deny the facts.

26. to depend on

abhängen von
abhängig sein von } to be dependent on
sich verlassen auf + acc — to rely on, to be certain about

Success doesn't always
depend on hard work.

A country's prosperity
depends on its exports.

You can always depend
on him.

Some people depend
too much on others.

Note:

That depends. — *Das/Es kommt darauf an.*

27. different

anders (als) — different from s.o. or s.th. else
(only predicatively)
verschieden — differing from each other
(predicatively and attributively)

That's quite different!

His four sons were all
very different.

The colours of the flags
were all different.

The situation in this
country is different
from what I thought.

He's quite different
from his brother.

We have different
interests.

28. entrance

der Eingang — place for entering on foot
die Einfahrt — place for driving in

The entrance to the garage
was blocked by demon-
strators.

The three girls were
waiting at the entrance
to the underground.

The entrance to the
theatre was full of people.

We saw an accident near
the entrance to the docks.

29. even

sogar, selbst — even
nicht einmal — not even
noch + comparative — even more

After his illness, he worked even more slowly than before.

Even his closest friends were surprised at his decision.

Not even his own mother would recognize him.

It was so cold that even the river was frozen.

We didn't even have time for a cup of coffee.

This ring is even more valuable than the other one.

He will come even if he has to walk all the way.

30. to feel

überschreiten — to go beyond a limit
übertreffen — to surpass, to outdo, to be superior to

Driving to work, he
exceeded the speed limit.

The results exceeded
all expectations.

He exceeded the time limit
by 45 minutes.

This year's profits
have far exceeded those
of last year.

31. to feel

fühlen, spüren — to feel by touch, to sense
sich fühlen — to feel well, ill etc (physical or emotional state)
sich anfühlen — to give the impression of being

How do you feel?

He felt the gun in his back.

It felt wet.

I don't feel the cold at all.

The material felt like
leather.

Last night she felt better.

32. food

das Essen — food for persons
das Futter — food for animals

What was the food like in Germany?

The harvest was so bad, the farmers had no food for the cattle.

The food at that restaurant is good.

We never buy dog-food in tins.

Note:

essen } to eat (of persons)
fressen }   (of animals)

33. to gather

sammeln — to collect (things)
versammeln — to bring together (persons)
sich (ver)sammeln — to come together (persons)

The tourists gathered round the statue.

We went into the wood to gather berries.

The crowd gathered in front oft the town hall.

The journalist flew to Ghana to gather information on the country.

The teacher gathered the boys around him.

34. glass

das Glas (no plural form) — a fixed quantity of drink
das Glas, die Gläser — actual glass container

She brought him three
glasses from Murano as
a present.

Waiter, two glasses
of wine, please!

One often finds lovely
old glasses in museums.

He couldn't drink more
than three glasses of beer.

Note:

die Brille (sing) — glasses, spectacles

Where are my glasses?

35. to go

gehen — (in general, or in particular on foot)
fahren — (by car, bus, train etc)

Are you going to London
next week?

Jimmy isn't at home. He's
gone to the cinema.

In the summer, a lot of
people go to the seaside.

Go into the garden and
fetch some flowers, please.

Note:

spazierengehen — to go for a walk
zu Fuß gehen — to walk

I've got a flat tire;
I'll have to walk.

Do you want to go for a
walk this afternoon?

36. to hang

hängen (hängte, gehängt) — to fasten, to suspend
hängen (hing, gehangen) — to be fastened, to be suspended

She hung her coat
on a nail.

The washing was hanging
on the line to dry.

It was so cold, an icicle
hung down from his nose.

Every day he hung his
umbrella on the same hook.

Note:

to hang about — *herumstehen, -sitzen, -liegen*

These people are always
hanging about the market-
place.

37. here

hier

a particular place near the speaker (no movement)

hierher

to a particular place near the speaker (implies movement)

Do you work here?

Bring the records here!

I live here.

Come here!

Here's my room.

He's coming here today.

38. hot

heiß — hot in temperature
scharf — well-spiced

Is this mustard very hot?

Be careful, the plate is hot!

It's much too hot here.

In an Indian restaurant, I always order the hottest dish there is.

Note:

I am/feel hot. — *Mir ist heiß.*

39. if

wenn { in the case of
under the condition that

ob — whether

Could you tell me if he
is coming today?

If it's possible I shall
be there at 6 o'clock.

He asked me
if I could help.

If I had the money
I'd give it to you.

He will ring me up
if he can't come.

I don't know
if it's right.

40. to imagine

sich vorstellen — to picture s.th. or s.o.
sich einbilden — to have a mistaken belief
(often expressing conceit)

He imagines he knows
everything.

It's difficult to imagine
technological progress
without nuclear energy.

You can imagine
how surprised I was!

He imagines he's a
great actor.

I can't imagine what
he's doing.

Note:

imagination — *die Phantasie*

Haven't you got
any imagination?

41. to increase

steigen — to become greater (in number, size or degree)
steigern — to make greater

The population of the
world increases
from year to year.

During his speech,
the tension in the hall
increased.

Last year, production
was increased by 10 %.

The number of unemployed
increases in the winter.

Success increases
one's self-confidence.

42. just

genau — exactly, precisely

gerade, eben { at this/that moment
{ a short while ago

gerade/eben noch — just about, just within the limit

That's just what we need.

We were late,
the film had just started.

I've got just enough petrol
to get home.

The train's just leaving.

I've just told you!

I've got just enough money
to pay for it.

He always seems to have
just the right answer.

We have just talked
to him about it.

43. to keep

behalten — to keep (for oneself)
aufheben — to save s.th. for later

We keep the newspapers
for our neighbours.

You can keep the book,
I don't need it.

May I keep it?

Keep the rest for
tomorrow!

Note:

to keep + verb in continuous form — verb + *dauernd*

He keeps disturbing me.

44. to know

kennen + acc — to know a person/a place

wissen { + subordinate clause } to have knowledge of,
{ + acc } to know a fact

Do you know that he has
never lost a game?

I know that from my own
experience.

Do you know the young
lady over there?

He doesn't know how to
repair the washing-
machine.

36

He knew the town from his student days.

What do you know about him?

45. to leave

(weg)gehen, (ab)fahren — to go away
verlassen — to leave (a person, place etc)
hängen/liegen/stehen lassen — to leave behind, to forget
lassen — to allow s.o. or s.th. to remain in a particular place
 or state

Paul left his wife and went to sea.

May I leave my little poodle with you?

I've left my umbrella in the restaurant.

He left half an hour ago.

Please leave your luggage here!

When did he leave school?

My aunt left her false-teeth in the hotel.

He left the door open.

When does the train leave?

Note:

to leave a message — *eine Nachricht hinterlassen*
Leave it to me! — *Überlassen Sie es mir!*

46. to lie; to lie down

sich hinlegen — to lie down
sich legen — to lie down somewhere
liegen — to be in a lying position

You must lie down
for an hour!

I don't want to lie down!

It isn't very comfortable
to lie on the floor.

Please lie down on the
couch!

Thousands of holiday-
makers were lying on the
beach.

After breakfast they lay
down in the sun.

Note:

The verbs "to come" and "to go" in the expression
"to go/come and lie down" are often omitted in German.

I often go and lie down
after lunch.

47. light

hell — light to the eye

leicht { not heavy
not rich or strong (of food)

In summer I like to wear light shoes.

Light wine goes well with light food.

It's not light enough to read.

I prefer plastic buckets, they're lighter.

She was wearing a light-blue dress.

48. to live

leben { to spend (a part of) one's life
to have a way of life

wohnen — to have one's home

Where do you live?

After the war
he lived in America.

They're living
beyond their means.

All our friends
live out of town.

They live on the 2nd floor.

He's living under a false name.

49. to look

sehen, schauen — to look (in a certain direction)
aussehen — to have the appearance

Look who's coming!

He looks tired.

He looked as if he hadn't understood the question.

He just stood there looking through the window.

She looks as if she has won a million dollars.

Note:

ansehen, anschauen — to look at (s.o.)
sich etwas ansehen/anschauen — to look at s.th.

Look at that!

She looked at me.

50. to look + preposition

sorgen für — to look after (to take care of)
aufpassen (auf) + acc — to look after (to keep under control)
suchen (nach) — to look for
nachschlagen — to look up

What are you looking for?

Would you please look after my dog for a moment?

The Red Cross looked after the refugees.

If you don't know a word you must look it up.

In the evening a friend looked after the children.

Are you still looking for a room?

His nephew looked after him until he died.

51. to lose

verlieren { opposite of "to find"
opposite of "to win"

sich verirren — to lose one's way (generally)
sich verlaufen, sich verfahren — to lose one's way
(walking/driving)

I've lost my keys!

The little girl lost her
way in the crowd.

Some parents lose their
temper very easily.

He lost the last game.

It was so dark that the
driver lost his way.

Note:

to lose weight — *abnehmen*

The doctor advised him
to lose weight.

52. to marry; to be married

heiraten — to get married, to marry
verheiratet sein (mit) — to be married (i.e. not single)

Are you married?

Anne is marrying her old boss tomorrow.

They got married in Gretna Green.

I think it's terrible to be married to such a woman!

Note:

sich verloben (mit) — to get engaged
sich scheiden lassen (von) — to get divorced

53. to mean

bedeuten — to have the meaning
meinen — to have in mind
wollen + verb — to mean to do s.th.

Do you mean Mr or Mrs Miller?

I didn't mean to offend you.

Do you know what that means?

He didn't mean Europe in the geographical sense.

The word "Liebe" means "love".

I meant to give it to you yesterday, but I forgot.

54. to meet

treffen — to meet by chance
sich treffen (mit) — to meet by arrangement, to come together
abholen — to meet in order to accompany
kennenlernen — to get to know

You don't need a taxi.
I'll meet you at the airport.

They meet their friends
every Thursday at the
tennis club.

Last week I met him
in town.

The delegates meet
once a year.

Evening school is a good
opportunity to meet
other people.

My father met me at the
station.

On holiday, you often meet
people you know.

When he was 20, he met
his future wife.

55. to miss

verpassen — not to catch, reach, or meet
vermissen — to long for s.o. or s.th. not present

He arrived late because he
had missed the bus.

When he was in Germany,
he missed his English
breakfast.

She wrote that she missed him very much.

Were you really there? Then we must have just missed each other.

56. most(ly)

der, die, das meiste (with uncountables)
die meisten (with countables) } most, most of

am meisten (adv) — to the greatest degree
meistens, meist (adv) — usually, as a rule
äußerst (adv) — extremely

Most of the people had gone when we arrived.

My father spends most of the time in the garden.

What disturbs you most?

The smallest boy made the most noise.

He's mostly at the club when he's not working.

She was wearing a most valuable necklace.

We're mostly at home on Saturdays.

He left a most important message.

Most German newspapers are not independent.

Note: *zum größten Teil* — mostly, for the most part

57. to move

(sich) bewegen — to (be or) put in motion
umziehen — to move house

We have moved twice
in three years.

Don't move!

I can't move this cup-
board.

Our neighbours are moving
tomorrow.

We don't want to move
again.

I could hardly move.

58. music

die Musik — music in general
die Noten (pl) — music in written form

Everyone has his own idea
of good music.

Has anyone seen my
music?

Do you like classical
music?

She can't read music.

One of the violinists
had forgotten his music.

He's decided to study
music.

59. must; must not

müssen — must
nicht dürfen — must not

We must be very careful.

You mustn't cross the road
when the lights are red!

You mustn't do that!

You must see that film!

We must go now.

Note:

nicht müssen — not to have to

You don't have to be rich
to be happy.

We don't have to go if we
don't want to.

60. night

der Abend — evening (time between evening meal and bed-
time)
die Nacht — night (time between going to bed and getting up)

Before we were married,
we went to the cinema
almost every night.

He spent three nights
in a hotel.

It was so hot that he
couldn't sleep all night.

He works hard during the
day but he also has a lot
to do at night.

Note:

abends, jeden Abend — every evening (night)
nachts, jede Nacht — every night
in der Nacht — at night
heute abend — this evening, tonight
gestern abend — yesterday evening, last night
heute nacht — the night that has just passed, as well as the
night to come, i.e. "last night" and "tonight"

61. number

die Nummer — (used as a label, or to differentiate s.th. from other similar objects)

die Zahl { (specifying the size or quantity)
figure, e.g. in mathematics

die Anzahl — an unspecified number of a total quantity

The number is over the front door.

The number of victims is not yet known.

You'll find the number in the telephone directory.

A number of firms didn't want to pay the higher wages.

3, 5, and 7 are uneven numbers.

Note:

die Ziffer — arithmetical symbol, digit
das Zifferblatt — clock-face

The numbers on the adding-machine were difficult to read.

62. on

in — on (a bus, train, ship etc)
an — fixed to, in contact with
auf — on top of

There's no name
on the door.

Don't sit down
on that cold stone!

He met her on the train
to Frankfort.

I don't like pictures
on the walls.

I left my camera on
the bus.

Excuse me, you're
standing on my foot!

63. only

nur — merely (expresses a limited number or the restricted nature of s.th.)

erst {
only . . . so far, only . . . at the moment (implies an extension in the future)
not before, not earlier than
}

He only spoke to one
person all day.

I only got the letter
yesterday.

They've only been
learning French for a year.

She can't travel alone
yet, she's only
seven years old.

There is only one answer
to this question.

64. order

der Befehl — command
die Bestellung — goods ordered
die Reihenfolge — sequence

The old lady sent her order to the grocer's every Friday.

The names in the telephone directory are in alphabetical order.

The bookshop received a lot of orders from abroad.

The soldier obeyed the order without hesitation.

We noted the events in chronological order.

The captain gave the order to abandon ship.

Note:

in Ordnung — in (good) order
außer Betrieb — out of order

Are your papers in order?

The lift is out of order.

65. to prescribe

verschreiben — to prescribe a medicine or treatment
vorschreiben — to fix (a law, a course of action etc)

Did the doctor prescribe
anything for your cough?

Has the committee got the
prescribed number of
members?

Sleeping-tablets are often
prescribed unnecessarily.

These measures are
prescribed by law.

Note:

das Rezept — "prescription" as well as "recipe"

66. to put

stellen — to put in an upright position
legen — to put in a flat position
stecken — to stick into

He couldn't put
the key in the lock.

She put the magazines
away and turned on the
radio.

He put the book
back on the shelf.

Anne put the teapot
on the table.

He put his hands
in his pocket.

Where have you
put my gloves?

She put the money back
in her purse.

Put the bottles
on the floor, please!

Note:

to put on a dress/a suit etc — *sich ein Kleid/eine Jacke*
anziehen
to put on a hat/glasses — *sich den Hut/die Brille aufsetzen*

67. quiet(ly)

leise — not loud(ly)

ruhig { calm(ly), not excited (of people and events)
not busy (of places)

We live in a very quiet
part of the town.

The Rolls Royce is famous
for its quiet engine.

She speaks so quietly
you can't understand her.

The shopkeepers said
it was the quietest Satur-
day of the year.

He sat quietly in the arm-
chair and smoked his pipe.

68. to be ready

fertig sein (mit) — to be completed, finished
bereit sein (zu) — to be prepared, to be willing and in a
position to do s.th.

Aren't you ready yet?

He's always ready to help.

When he came home,
supper was ready.

The plane was ready
for take-off.

When will my car
be ready?

He's never ready
to admit a mistake.

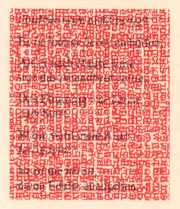

69. to realize

verwirklichen — to carry out, to make reality
(be)merken — to notice, to become suddenly aware of

It's easy to make plans
but difficult to realize
them.

After 5 minutes he realized
he wasn't alone.

They only realized it was
raining when they left
the house.

At last the government's
goals were realized.

70. to rent

mieten — to pay rent for the use of s.th.
vermieten — to receive rent for the use of s.th.

He rents rooms to
students.

Do you want to buy the
house or rent it?

It's very expensive to
rent a house in this
part of town.

Some people rent their
houses to tourists.

We rented a car during
the summer holidays.

71. rich

reich — wealthy
schwer — heavy (of food)

A rich uncle can be
extremely useful.

The rich get richer and
the poor get poorer.

The doctor advised the
patient to avoid rich food.

Rich and poor people
rarely live in the same
area.

This cake is too rich
for me.

72. to ride

fahren (mit) — to ride on/in a vehicle
reiten — to ride a horse or other animal

I go riding every Sunday
and Wednesday.

In summer, I ride to work
on my bike.

When we were in Egypt, we
rented a camel and rode
to the pyramids.

Some people enjoy riding
in a bus.

He jumped onto his horse
and rode off.

Note: to ride a bike — *radfahren*

73. room

der Platz (no plural form) — space, room to put things
das Zimmer — room, mainly in a private house
der Raum — room in general, usually large

Have you got any room for
my luggage in your car?

Our flat has only got two
rooms.

We rent a room in a pub
for our club evenings.

This room is much too
small!

There's no room for my
overcoat in the suitcase.

The rooms of the new
library are very modern
but there will soon be no
more room for new books.

Note:

der Platz, die Plätze { a place to sit
public square, (market)place

74. to save

sparen — to save money, time etc
retten — to rescue

I can't save anything
on my present salary.

All the passengers were
saved.

We were saved by our
safety-belts.

If we drive slower
we'll save a lot of petrol.

The dog saved his life.

Note:

Save me a piece of cake
please!

That will save you
a lot of trouble.

75. seat

der Sitz — s.th. for sitting on
            (a particular seat)
der Platz — a place to sit
            (general)

Please take a seat!

In this car even the
back-seat is comfortable.

We've booked two seats
for the theatre tonight.

A new seat has been
developed for pilots.

76. to see

sehen — to see (in general)
verstehen — to understand
besuchen — to go/come and see
sprechen mit jdm (über) — to see s.o. (about)

Can you see the ship
on the horizon?

I'm going to see him
tomorrow.

Do you see what I mean?

He could see nothing at
all.

You can't see the doctor
now.

Later, I saw why he had
done it.

What do you want to see
the manager about?

It would be nice if you
could come and see me
at the weekend.

77. to sit; to sit down

sitzen — to be seated
sich setzen — to take a seat, to sit down

They sat round the table
all evening
and played cards.

I could sit here
for hours!

The dog suddenly stopped
barking and sat down
in front of the door.

When the police came,
the demonstrators were
still sitting in the road.

Thomas sat down on
Grandfather's knee.

Sit down please!

Note:

The committee sat for ten hours. — Das Komitee *tagte* zehn
Stunden.

78. skin

die Haut — skin of a human being or animal with no fur
das Fell — animal skin with fur
die Schale — skin of fruits or vegetables (which are normally peeled)

Babies have a very
sensitive skin.

Rabbit skins are
relatively cheap.

We were wet to the skin.

The skin of this apple
is very tough.

Reindeer skins are
exported from Lapland.

Don't throw the banana
skin out of the window!

79. so

so — so + adj or adv — to such an extent; very
darum, deshalb — for that reason
es — (as substitute for a phrase)

It was late, so we took
a taxi.

Is he coming tomorrow?
I suppose so.

We were so happy.

How do you know he did it?
My wife said so.

He didn't know,
so he asked me.

Don't be so nervous!

Note:

I think so. — *Ich glaube ja.*
I don't think so. — *Ich glaube nein/nicht.*

80. some

etwas — a little (for uncountables)
einige — a few (for countables)

I need some money.

He has got some
beautiful old books.

Would you like some
coffee?

Some of the guests
stayed till midnight.

81. to spend

ausgeben — to spend money
verbringen — to spend time

My father had to spend six months in a sanatorium last year.

Do you know that Eva has spent £50 on new clothes this week?

Where are you going to spend your holidays this year?

Although he earns a lot, he doesn't spend much.

82. to spoil

verderben {
  to make bad
  to become bad
}
verwöhnen — to spoil a person

The food is spoilt.

Richard has always been spoilt by his grandparents.

Fresh fish spoil easily.

His wife likes to spoil him.

Don't spoil your appetite!

83. to start

beginnen, anfangen — to commence
losgehen } to depart   (on foot)
losfahren }   (in vehicles)

When he was 70, he started to learn Russian.

We had a long journey before us, so we had to start early.

When do you start work?

I'll have to start at 6 o'clock to be there on time.

Note:

Ich konnte den Motor nicht *starten/anlassen.* — I couldn't start the engine.
Das Flugzeug *startete* pünktlich. — The plane took off on time.

84. step(s)

der Schritt — a pace (also figuratively)
die Stufe — step (e.g. of a staircase)
die Treppe — steps, stairs

Mind the step!

What steps have been taken to find him?

The water became deeper at every step.

The steps led into the wine-cellar.

That's a big step forward!

He took three steps at a time as he rushed up the steps to the school.

Note:

step by step — *Schritt für Schritt*

85. to stop

aufhören — to cease, to discontinue

stehenbleiben { to stop walking / to stop functioning }

halten — to come to a halt (of vehicles)
anhalten — to bring to a halt
hindern — to prevent

After six weeks I stopped learning German.

She tried to stop other cars in order to get help.

It's dangerous to stop on the motorway.

The rain has stopped at last!

We can't stop him going to court.

The clock stopped in the middle of the night.

The bus doesn't stop here.

You can't stop me talking!

The little girl stopped in front of every shop window.

The sports car was stopped by the police.

86. suspicious

mißtrauisch, argwöhnisch — having a suspicion
verdächtig — causing suspicion

The whole story was
rather suspicious.

A detective must be
suspicious by nature.

At that time, the police
weren't suspicious.

His behaviour seems very
suspicious to me.

He trusts nobody.
He's very suspicious.

87. to swear

schwören — to take an oath, to pledge
fluchen — to curse, to use bad language

Can your parrot swear,
too?

I swear I've never seen
him before.

He had to swear that he
would never speak to
anyone about it.

Stop swearing!

Note:

Can you swear to that? — *Kannst du das beschwören?*

88. to take

nehmen — to take (in general)
bringen — to take to a specified place (away from the speaker)
dauern — to take time

How long will it take?

She took another piece of cake.

Would you take this parcel to the post-office, please?

The injured were taken to hospital.

The operation took three hours.

Have you taken your medicine?

Note:

Is this seat taken? — Ist dieser Platz *besetzt?*
How many photos have you taken? — Wieviele *Fotos* haben Sie *gemacht?*

89. that

der, die, das (with noun)
     das (without noun) } (demonstrative)
der, die, das — (relative pronoun)
daß — (conjunction)

Have you read the novel
that I gave you?

Is that your car?

He said that he would help
me if he could.

I wouldn't buy that car.

It was so hot that we
couldn't sleep all night.

I don't believe that story!

That's a good idea!

The only book that really
interests him is his
cheque-book.

90. then

dann — after that
damals — at that time

They spent a week in
Madrid and then went on
to Lisbon.

We were all beginners
then.

As a child, I often swam
in this lake; the water was
still clean then.

We had supper and then
went for a walk.

91. there

da/dort  in that place
(no movement)
dahin/dorthin to that place
(implies movement)

There he is!

Why aren't you going
there?

My brother was there.

Put the suitcase there,
please.

92. there is/are

es gibt + acc — (expressing existence, not pointing to
                              anyone or anything specific)

es ist/sind + nom
nom + *ist/sind* } (pointing to s.o. or s.th. specific)

There's no water on the
moon.

There's a fly in the soup!

There are still some storks
in Northern Germany.

There's no-one there.

Is there another
possibility?

Note:

More specific verbs (e.g. *stehen, liegen* etc) are often used
instead of *sein*.

There was a bus in front of
the house when I got home.

There was a big cat
on his bed.

93. to think

denken an + acc — to direct one's thoughts towards
nachdenken (über) + acc — to ponder over, to think about
halten von — to have an opinion on

What do you think about it?

He always thought of the girl he loved.

He thought about the problem for a long time.

I thought about her plans for a long time.

They don't think much of their new boss.

A mother always thinks of her children first.

Note:

1. *sich überlegen* — often instead of *nachdenken über*, particularly when the object does not need to be specified and is expressed by *es* or *das*.

   I must think about it. — Ich muß *darüber nachdenken.*/
   Ich muß *mir das überlegen.*

2. I can't think of it at the moment. — Es *fällt* mir im Augenblick nicht *ein*.

94. time

die Zeit — time (generally)
das Mal — occasion

I'll pay next time.

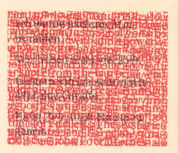

We haven't got much time.

Yesterday I saw a giraffe
for the first time.

It's time to go home.

Note:

einmal, zweimal, dreimal etc — once, twice, three times etc

He's told you five times
already.

95. to

nach — (to countries without the definite article in the name
and towns)
in — (to countries with the definite article in the name)
zu — (to persons and particular places)

My brother is going to
Hamburg today.

The little girl ran to her
mother.

Germany exports a lot of
cars to Switzerland.

The senator is flying back
to the United States
tomorrow.

A lot of Americans go to France.

She accompanied me to the station.

Note:

ins Kino — to the cinema
ins Konzert — to a concert
ins Theater — to the theatre

96. to treat

behandeln { to handle
{ to treat an illness/a sick person
einladen — to supply s.th. at one's own expense, to invite

May I treat you to a beer?

He treated her like a child.

You can't treat tuberculosis with penicillin.

Michael has always treated his dog well.

His uncle treated him to a visit to the zoo.

Which doctor is treating you?

97. to try

versuchen — to attempt
probieren — to sample, to try s.th. out

We are trying
to improve our German.

Would you like to try
my cake?

I should like to try
a different sort this time.

He tries to understand
her problems.

98. to use

benutzen — to make use of
verbrauchen — to use up
mit etw umgehen (können) — (to know how) to use s.th.

I don't know how to use
that mixer.

Have you used all the
paper?

My grandmother never
used a vacuum-cleaner.

We haven't used much oil
this winter.

Do you use
an electric razor?

Do you know how to use
the tape-recorder?

99. to wake (up)

aufwachen — to awake
(auf)wecken — to wake s.o. up

When shall I wake you
(up)?

I woke up four times
in the night.

I'm not going to wake you
(up) any more in the
morning; buy your-self an
alarm-clock.

Don't wake him (up)!

Wake up, it's time to go!

The baby always wakes up
early in the morning.

100. when

wann — at what time (in questions and subordinate clauses)
als — at the time when (only in the past; referring to a single
 incident)

wenn
{ whenever
{ at the time when (in the future)

When have you got time?

I don't know when I
shall see her again.

When I talk about that,
he changes the subject.

When she arrived home,
she found the door open.

Did he say
when he would come?

He's always there
when I need him.

When the boss tells a joke,
everybody has to laugh.

When do you want to
go home?

We can give it to him
when he comes.

When he was young,
everything was different.

101. where

wo — where (no movement)
wohin, wo . . . hin — where to (implies movement)

Where do you live?

Where are you going?

I don't know where I've
left my watch.

Charles knows where they
have taken it.

Where's Richard?
Do you know where
he went?

Note:

woher, wo . . . her — where from

Where does he come from?

102. words

die Worte — words in context
die Wörter — single words

Nobody can learn all the
words of a language.

It's sometimes difficult
to find the right words.

How many words has the
German language got?

His last words were,
"There's a hole in the
bucket."

103. to work

arbeiten — to do work
funktionieren
gehen (for mechanical devices) } to function, to operate

Nobody knows how
the brain works.

My friend works on a farm.

How does that work?

You must knock; the bell
doesn't work.

We've never seen him
work.

Note: to work out — *ausrechnen*

Stumbling Blocks

Not only but also

to enjoy	a) *sich amüsieren* (oneself) b) *genießen* (something)
excuse	a) *Entschuldigung* (true) b) *Ausrede* (invented)
to float	a) *schwimmen* (not to sink) b) *treiben* (to move along in water)
hard	a) *hart* b) *schwer* (as in: *schwere Arbeit, schwer zu lösen*)
how	a) *wie* b) *woher* (in: *Woher wissen Sie das?*)
to be late	a) *spät sein* b) *zu spät kommen* (after agreed time)
line	a) *Linie* b) *Zeile* (in a book)
pilot	a) *Pilot* (plane) b) *Lotse* (ship)
platform	a) *Plattform* b) *Bahnsteig* (in a station)
to stand	a) *stehen* b) *ertragen, vertragen* (to bear)

Similar words with different meanings

key: ≠ not the same as
      ↓ means

brave	≠	*brav*
↓		↓
mutig, tapfer		well-behaved
eventually	≠	*eventuell*
↓		↓
schließlich		perhaps
fatal	≠	*fatal*
↓		↓
tödlich		awful, unfortunate
genial	≠	*genial*
↓		↓
freundlich		brilliant
meaning	≠	*Meinung*
↓		↓
Bedeutung		opinion
ordinary	≠	*ordinär*
↓		↓
normal		common, vulgar
to overhear	≠	*überhören*
↓		↓
zufällig hören		not to hear
sensible	≠	*sensibel*
↓		↓
vernünftig		sensitive
sympathetic	≠	*sympathisch*
↓		↓
mitfühlend		pleasant, friendly

Different gender different meaning

der Band, ⸚e	volume (book)
das Band, ⸚er	tape, ribbon
der Bauer, -n	farmer
das Bauer, -	birdcage
der Erbe, -n	heir
das Erbe, die Erbschaften	heritage/inheritance
der Gehalt	contents
das Gehalt, ⸚er	salary
der Heide, -n	pagan, heathen
die Heide	heather
der Kiefer, -	jaw
die Kiefer, -n	pine-tree
der Schild, -e	shield
das Schild, -er	sign, notice
der See, -n	lake
die See	sea
das Steuer	steering-wheel
die Steuer, -n	tax
der Tau	dew
das Tau, -e	rope
der Verdienst	income
das Verdienst, -e	merit
der Weise, -n	sage, wise man
die Weise, -n	way (method)

Solutions to Test-sentences (p. 4/5)

The number in brackets after each word indicates the corresponding English headword.

1. bat (10)
2. ändern (21)
3. in (95)
4. anders (27)
5. Zahl (61)
6. hierher (37)
7. gehört (14)
8. nachdem (3)
9. Eingang (28)
10. ob (39)
11. vorstellen (40)
12. gerade/eben (42)
13. kennen (44)
14. erst (63)
15. verheiratet (52)
16. wohnen (48)
17. treffen uns (54)
18. dauern (88)
19. verschrieben (65)
20. stellen (66)
21. Platz (73)
22. vermietet (70)
23. dürfen . . . nicht (59)
24. versuchten (97)
25. gespart (74)
26. stehengeblieben (85)
27. verlassen (45)
28. vor (13)
29. wann (100)
30. über . . . nachdenken (93)
31. wecken (99)
32. etwas (80)
33. wohin (101)
34. nennen (19)
35. bringen (88)
36. hell (47)
37. funktioniert/geht (103)
38. es waren (92)
39. vorsichtig (20)
40. kümmern (11)
41. (ver)sammelten sich (33)
42. leider (2)
43. noch einmal (4)
44. außer (17)
45. von (18)
46. bedeutet (53)
47. Platz (75)
48. verstehe (76)
49. es (79)
50. dahin/dorthin (91)

List of German Words

The numbers refer to the English headwords, except when
there is a p. (= page) in front.

Eine Reihe für den Deutschlernenden:

Lesen leicht gemacht

Einfache oder vereinfachte Texte aus der deutschen Literatur,
die Freude am Lesen wecken
und die Kenntnisse der deutschen Sprache und Literatur erweitern.

Leicht	Klettbuch
Christian Bock, *Das sonderbare Telefon*	55914
Christian Bock, *Seltsames Verhör*	55913
Wolf Durian, *Kai aus der Kiste*	55923
Max von der Grün, *Die Entscheidung (Erzählungen)*	55928
Peter Härtling, *Das war der Hirbel*	55924
Wilhelm Hauff, *Märchen aus dem Orient*	55927
Joe Lederer, *Drei Tage Liebe*	55912
Ludwig Thoma, *Lausbubengeschichten*	55919

Leicht bis mittelschwer	
Christian Bock, *Das Schlafwagenabteil*	55915
A. von Chamisso, *Peter Schlemihls wundersame Geschichte*	55922
Friedrich Gerstäcker, *Die Flucht über die Kordilleren*	55921
E. T. A. Hoffmann, *Das Fräulein von Scuderi*	55911
Gottfried Keller, *Romeo und Julia auf dem Dorfe*	55917
Siegfried Lenz, *Ein Haus aus lauter Liebe (Erzählungen)*	55916
Joachim Maass, *Der Fall de la Roncière*	55925
Charles Sealsfield (Karl Postl), *Der Kapitän*	55918
Theodor Weißenborn, *Der Sprung ins Ungewisse*	55926

Die Reihe wird fortgesetzt.

Ernst Klett Verlag Stuttgart